MANAGING

INFORMATION AND THE FUTURE

Gana Kiritharan

WWW.GKIRI.COM

MANAGING INFORMATION AND THE FUTURE

By Gana Kiritharan

For contact information please visit: www.gkiri.com

ISBN:
E-Book: 978-1-894727- 04-4
Soft Cover: 978-1-894727- 02-0
Lulu Edition: 978-1-894727- 05-1

Published by:-

Gana Kiritharan
    Canada
www.gkiri.com

CONTENTS

5. The Information of Worksite

6. Managing the Change and the Future

Chapter One

INTRODUCTION

1.1 DREAMS VERSUS REALITY

Human civilization and Management function are going through rapid changes with unexpected turns and twists. At the end of the last century human civilization was dreaming about information revolution and consequently economic prosperity. There was enthusiasm about the information superhighway and internet. Intellectuals were dreaming about and calculating sustained economic growth for the next 25 years and alleviation of social problems by the information management system. When everybody was waiting for the economic slowdown which started around the beginning of this century to get reversed, September 11 terror attacks on America came as a blow to every dream. September 11 attacks may not be the only cause of the problem. It may be necessary to consider financial scandals in large American companies, continuing high oil prices and still unexplained philosophical reasons for economic slowdown and recession as reasons for this continuing problem.

Fig 1.1: Dreams and Reality

Despite all these challenges there is expectation about economic growth and prosperity in the future. Investments are still being made on improving information superhighway and it is still considered that buying a personal computer is a better personal investment for future. If all these expectation are true information revolution is sooner or later going to break all its barriers and going to lead human civilization towards a better future and social relationship. In the past information revolution has shown that it is not going to stop it effect with certain parts of technical process or just with analog and digital calculations for which computers were initially invented. Almost all parts of social life are going to change at various levels by this revolution. One of the important aspects of the society that is going to be changed by computerization is management practice and decision-making process.

1.2 INFORMATION AND MANAGEMENT

Nowadays seeing a management office without computers or manager without computer knowledge is becoming increasingly impossible. Managers are using computers well beyond their initial use of word processing and financial management. Usually managers' computers are connected to employees' attendance sheet to schedule and quality management data bases of production line.

Fig 1.2: Computers and Managers

Beyond this managers are using computers to access important information from internet for their business purposes. Maintaining own websites and giving emails address becoming more easy and professional way of running business and maintaining business contacts. What are the advantages and disadvantages of computerization and information revolution is a big subject-matter of discussion. At least as managers we know that if we do not know anything about computers then we cannot survive in the information revolution.

This book introduces and explains a detailed definition of information, how computers help us to access and analyze this information. In chapter two I will define and explain what we mean by the word information and in chapter three I will explain in detail about computers. Chapter four will explain about computerization and social challenges faced on computerization and chapter five will explain important information which can be gathered from the work site and how this information can be organized and analyzed using computerized information management system. In chapter six I will summarize and explain important changes due to information revolution, how to manage these changes and the future.

Chapter Two

INFORMATION

2.1 DEFINITION OF INFORMATION

Defining information or giving detailed explanation for it which is acceptable for all educational disciplines may not be an easy target. Each educational discipline will try to have a comfortable definition for them. As the matter of discussion of this book is how computers help us to analyze information it is better to define information on that basis. In computer science the most popular way of programming information management software is called Object Oriented Programming. Let us try to have a detailed understanding of the object and object-oriented programming.

The world is made of several objects and functions which directly or indirectly influence other objects and existence. Before going into a detailed discussion of these objects, it become essential to understand in what context the word object is used in this discussion. As information management software is designed to collect information regarding individuals, groups, institutions even inanimate objects, process or functions, it is necessary to include all the above within the word "object". For example the software designed for banking accounts is actually designed for a function or procedure. In computer science it becomes necessary to include that function as an object for further understanding of its performance. Again the objects in an environment may be grouped under different categories. It may be people, inanimate objects, tools, machines, functions, procedures may be some example for these groups. All these objects and groups influence other objects and groups directly or indirectly.

Fig 2.1 Objects in a Production Environment

The next task is defining and explaining these objects in detail. In an environment when you can identify and define something uniquely and differentiate it from other components of environment then it can be considered to be an object. These objects have certain properties which helps to identify them and differentiate them from other objects in the environment. For an example you are working in a production line of computers, the possible identifiable objects in that environment includes people, tables, chairs, assembly tracts, tools and computer components. In this environment even though they are physically not identifiable the procedures you are following can be identified differently by it function from other objects. So they also need to be considered as separate objects.

2.2 OBJECTS AND PROPERTIES

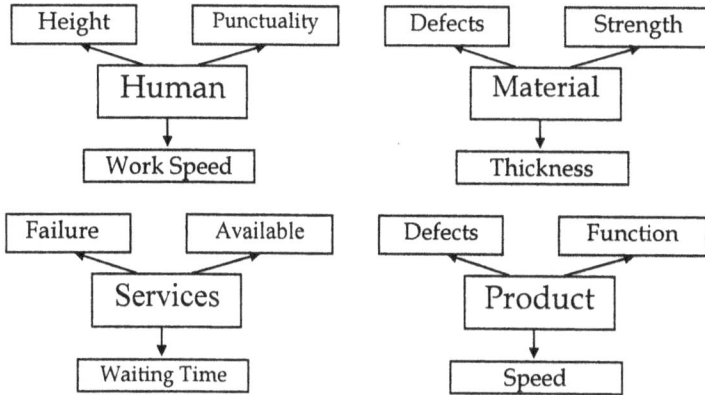

Fig 2.2 Objects and Properties

When some of these objects have certain properties which are common to these then they can be considered to be a group. People for example have properties common for everybody so that they can be grouped into one. These common properties help us to differentiate people from other objects like furniture or tools. The furniture, tools, computer components and procedures can be grouped into different groups. Within the group we use certain other properties to differentiate objects with one another. For an example we use height and facial appearance of people to differentiate between them. We gave identification number to differentiate one procedure from another.

These properties when measured should vary between objects. Then only it will help us to differentiate the objects. Because they vary they are given another term "variable". Variable is a mathematical term commonly used in computer programming. Variable by definition is a property, when measured varying between objects. Though it is not that important it is better to mention here the mathematical term used opposite to variable is "constant". Constant by definition is a property, when measured does not vary between objects. Numbers of fingers, for example, do not vary between people so that it is a constant. Though constant does not help us to differentiate between objects within one group or class, it may help us to differentiate one group from another.

2.3 DATA, INFORMATION AND KNOWLEDGE

These variables and constants can be stored in computers as pieces of information and used in analyzing and reporting. When storing in computers these variables are given a more technical term "data" and according to the type of measurement they can be defined as various "data types". Data is a piece of information with definite value but little meaning. When the data get analyzed, summarized and arranged in a logical order, it gives a useful idea about the object it is called information. For example following is a list of data, Planet A, Light Bulb, 23 Employees, Week 32, 108 Good Products and 12 Bad Products. All above data give us definite values but we could get little meaning from them. If we can arrange the above data as follows, then they will give us a more meaningful idea. "Twenty three employees are working in a production line of light bulbs in Plant A, in week 32 they produced 108 good products and 12 bad products." Above sentence give us a useful idea so that it is information. Chapter three will explain in detail how this information stored and analyzed in computers.

Before the discussion about computers it is more useful to have a basic understanding of some more words related to information. When a considerable amount of information about an object presented in an organized and logical manner, another term given is knowledge. By definition knowledge means information gathered from a formal presentation or education and presented in formal manner. The word "common sense" is used more for information gathered from experience not by formal education. Knowledge and common sense are essential for performing any kind of job. Though knowledge can be defined, written in procedure and can be instituted through formal education, common sense comes from gathering and sharing experience.

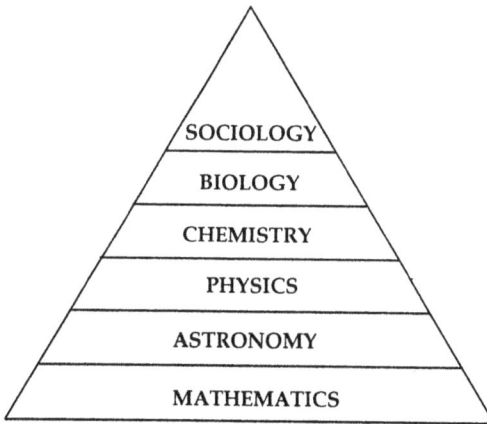

Fig 2.4: Comet's Hierarchy of Sciences

There are several different ways of classifying of knowledge field. The basic way of classification comes from Auguste Comet (1798 – 1857), the person who is considered to be the father of sociology. He organized the basic knowledge fields according to increasing complexity in a pyramid shape. According to him mathematics which is a less complex one gets placed on the bottom of the pyramid and sociology the more complex one placed on the top of the pyramid.

With his basic understanding about information and related fields let start the discussion about computers and how information is stored and analyzed by computers.

Chapter Three

COMPUTERS

3.1 INTRODUCTION

Computers are basically a microelectronic system which receives input, perform some predefined process for the input and provide the output. A microelectronic system which is the basic architecture of a microcomputer system contains input devices to receive the information from the environment, microprocessor to perform necessary process to the information and output devices to perform the output. The microprocessor will be connected to a program memory where it stores all the necessary information to perform its function.

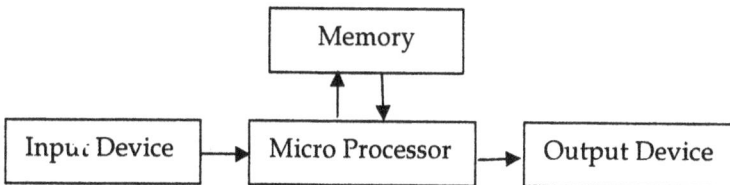

Fig 3.1 Microelectronic System

Any computer whether small or large needs two different components for its functions. First one is Hardware next one is Software. The word hardware means all the physical components of computers. Video Display Unit, a TV screen like part; Keyboard, a typewriter-like part; System Unit, a box-like part where hard drive, floppy disk drive and all-important chips are held together and every other physical components joined to the computer are called hardware. Even if they are connected properly all the above mentioned hardware are not capable of working alone. They need electronic instructions to perform each function.

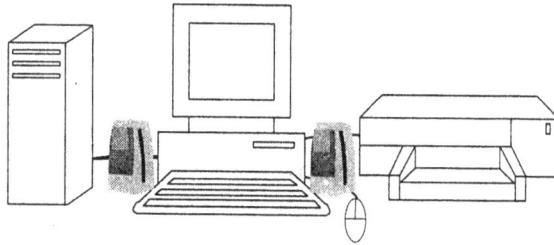

Fig 3.2 Computer Hardware

3.2 SOFTWARE

These electronic instructions which are written in different computer languages called software. These software instructions and information are stored in different kinds of computer disks and provided with the hardware. In these disks information is stored in a format, which can be read by the computers. This information contains instructions for the computer to perform each task. Usually these programs will be stored in the hard disk at first instance, and later the computer will start and work without these disks. Software can be grouped into three major categories according to their function.

3.2.1 Operating System

These are the basic and important instructions necessary for the functions of a computer. Operating system will connect and control different devices like video display unit, mouse, printer and keyboard to the main system. In addition operating system will regulate the information we are going to store in the computer. Without installing an operating system, you cannot go any further in using the computer. Commonly used operating systems are MS-DOS, WINDOWS, UNIX, SUN operating system etc.

3.2.2 Compiler Software

Actually computers are not capable of understanding languages talked by humans. They only understand and communicate with each part by electronic signals, which are known as machine language. But you know that the instructions we are giving to the computers from keyboard or by mouse on screen are in one of the languages we commonly speak and understand. The software that helps the computer to understand the instruction is a compiler. It works as translator and translates the instruction from human language to machine language and from machine language to human language. Whenever you try to install a program on your computer the compiler will be installed automatically and starts to work as translator between the program and the hardware. Examples for compiler software are C complier for programs written in C language, Pascal compiler for programs written in Pascal language.

3.2.3 Application Software

This is the most important part for a common user of a computer. These are programs written to perform certain tasks for the users. It may be typing a letter, billing in a counter or accounting and so on. There are different kinds for different purposes. Most commonly used application software are Word Processors, Spreadsheets, Presentation Software and DBMS.

- Word processors, which are used for typing, editing and printing simple office letters to small booklets. Example for word processors are word Perfect, Word and Microsoft Word.
- Spreadsheets used to state mainly numerical data in the form of rows and columns. They allow you to perform detail analysis and calculations on numerical data. Some of the popular spreadsheet packages are lotus 1-2-3, Quattro Pro and MS Excel.
- Presentation software used to create professional quality presentations, which can be reproduced on transparency paper, 35 mm slides, and photo print and on screen presentations. Example for presentations software is MS Power Point.
- Database Management systems [DBMS] used to store not only numerical data but data in different formats. In DBMS you can store text, numbers, date, pictures, sound and video images and so on. Examples for DBMS are FoxPro, Clipper, MS Access and Oracle.

The four types of software discussed above are collectively called office packages, because they are used for better functions of office not only in business but also in every other type of organization. Even though the first three word processors, spreadsheet and presentation software are giving good help to run business, the last one Data Base Management Systems are the most important from the viewpoint of information management. Only DBMS can give convenient software to store and analyze different types of data. Before looking into DBMS in more detail, let see what the important functions of a computer are.

3.3 FUNCTIONS OF A COMPUTER

Today computers help mankind in many different ways, from running our washing machines to helping to launch and maintain satellites. So obviously computers have to perform many different functions. At least for our learning purpose, it may be possible for us to group these functions in the following categories.

3.3.1 Repetition

Computers are capable of doing repetitive functions very accurately in high speed. It may be printing a letter again and again or controlling a machine which does things repeatedly. When humans are asked to do such a job, it not only causes fatigue but also results in more errors as they proceed. But computers can do such tasks with very good diligence.

3.3.2 Arithmetic Calculations

Another important function computers can perform for us is arithmetic calculations. This may be performed by small calculators for simple arithmetic or by a super computer for weather forecast. Computers are capable of doing arithmetic calculations at high speed with better accuracy.

3.3.3 Information Management

This is the most important function computers are performing from the quality management point of view. Computers are capable of storing many different kinds of information and allow to retrieve this information for further use in whatever format that is required. As discussed earlier, the software used for information management system is Data Base Management system. When these DBMS follow certain standards, rules and regulations, they are known as Relational Data Base Management System.

3.3.4 Decision Making

Even though computers are capable of doing the above three functions on a more superior level than a human being, when coming to decision-making function computers are lying much further back than the human brain. Several attempts have been made to use computers in decision-making but unfortunately they are only capable up to the level they are instructed. Even a slightly different situation makes computers either produce erroneous results or abandon the task altogether. It is not known whether it is good or bad that computers do not have the capability of decision-making. At least for the time being, it is better to leave this task to human intelligence.

3.4 DATA BASE MANAGEMENT SYSTEM

As we have seen earlier, it is the most important subject a management person likes to know in computer science. It gives a convenient platform for managers where they can store different kind of information like employees' attendance to their photos and utilize such information in management function. A Data Base Management System is essentially a collection of interrelated data and a set of programs to access this data. Usually DBMS offers the following services.

- Data Definition: It is a method of defining data types that need to be stored.
- Data Maintenance: It checks whether each record has fields containing all information.
- Data Manipulation: Allows data in the database to be inserted updated deleted and sorted.
- Data Display: This helps in viewing data.

- Data Integrity: This ensures accruing of the data.

When a DBMS meets certain standards of American National Standard Institution [ANSI] it is called Relational DBMS [RDBMS]. An RDBMS can support a common computer language called structured quarry language [SQL]. With the help of SQL you can create a database, maintain data in it and revise necessary information whenever you need. Examples for RDBMS are Oracle, Sybase, SQL Server, and DB2 etc.

A database is made up of data and associated objects. Data base object includes tables, queries, forms, and reports. Let study these data base objects in some more detail.

3.4.1 Tables

MACHINE ID	TYPE	MANUFACTURER	DATE OF PURCHASE
9801	Cutter	TATA	JAN 1998
9802	Cutter	JAMAHA	JAN 1998
9803	Driller	JAMAHA	FEB 1998

Table 3.1 Table of Machines.

The information stored in a database is in the form of one or more tables. The tables are created in the format of row and column. Each table in a database focuses on one different type of information. There will be one table for information about the process, another table for information about the machines another table for information about customers and so on . 3.1 gives you a possible table of information about some machines.

Each table is divided into several rows and columns. Each row contains information about different machines. A single row with all of its information is called a record. Fields in a table are the columns of information. For example in Tab 3.1 third field from left field contains information about manufacturer. So, fields store a particular type of information. Every specific piece of information in a table is known as a value. Thus TATA is a value, Jan 1998 is a value and so on.

3.4.2 Forms

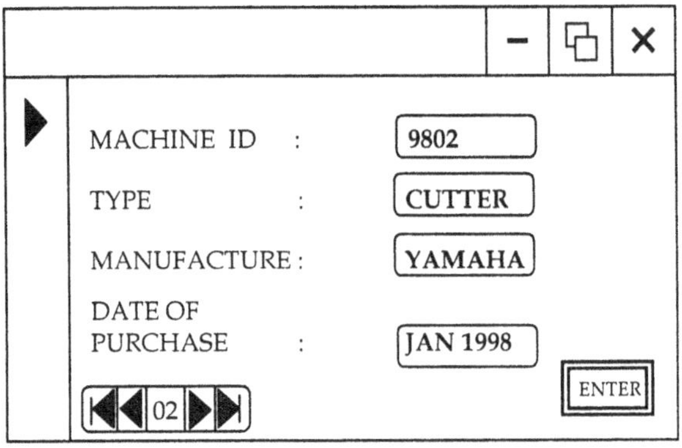

Fig 3.3 A Sample Form.

Forms help users to enter information into a database table in an easy and accurate manner. More than entering data into the tables you can also change, delete or view database records. You can use data- entry forms to restrict access to certain fields within a table. You can also use these forms to check the validity of the data before they are being accepted into database. For example you can ensure that "manufacturer" fields are not left blank; "Data of Purchase" entered in Month Year format. It is also possible to allow selective display of certain fields within the given table. By displaying selected fields, you can limit a users' access to sensitive data.

3.4.3 Queries

Queries are used to extract information from a database. A query can select a group of records that fulfill certain conditions with specified fields. An example of a query is when you want to see the list of machines produced by "YAMAHA" company. The Result of such query on table 3.1 may be as in table 3.2

MACHINE ID	TYPE	MANUFACTURER	DATE OF PURCHAES
9802	Cutter	JAMAHA	JAN 1998
9803	Driller	JAMAHA	FEB 1998

Table 3.2 Results of Query To select information
about YAMAHA machine.

Out of the four database objects we see here that a good understanding about queries will help quality management persons to analyze information about defects. In chapter five we will see some simple queries on a sample database. If you get a chance to learn about DBMS and queries, it will certainly help you in your management work.

3.4.4   Reports

Reports present your data in a printed format. You can create different types of reports with a DBMS. For example, your report can list all the records in a given table such as a list of all machines. You can even generate a report that lists only selective records, such as machines, purchased on JAN 1998. You can do this by incorporating a query within the report. Your reports can also combine multiple tables to present complex relationships among different sets of data. When you design your database, remember the information that you will need in future. Doing so ensures that all the information you require in your reports is easily available. Usually DBMS have facility of printing reports as figures or graphics. For example Pareto Charts, Pie charts and so on.

ABC ENTERPRISES

Adaptor Department

Weekly Production Report

Week No:- 04 (25/01/2004 – 31/01/2004)

Production Summery

Week	Quantity	Quality
19	20,855	93.5%
20	21,035	94%
21	22,005	93%
22	20,065	92%
23	22,345	93.5%

Best Performing Employees

Quantity	Quality
V. S. Singh – 3,850	D. Amirtharaj – 96.5%
M. Abdul – 3,605	S. Sukula – 96.3%
S. Pandian – 3,250	R. Singh – 95.9%

Department Manager   Department Engineer

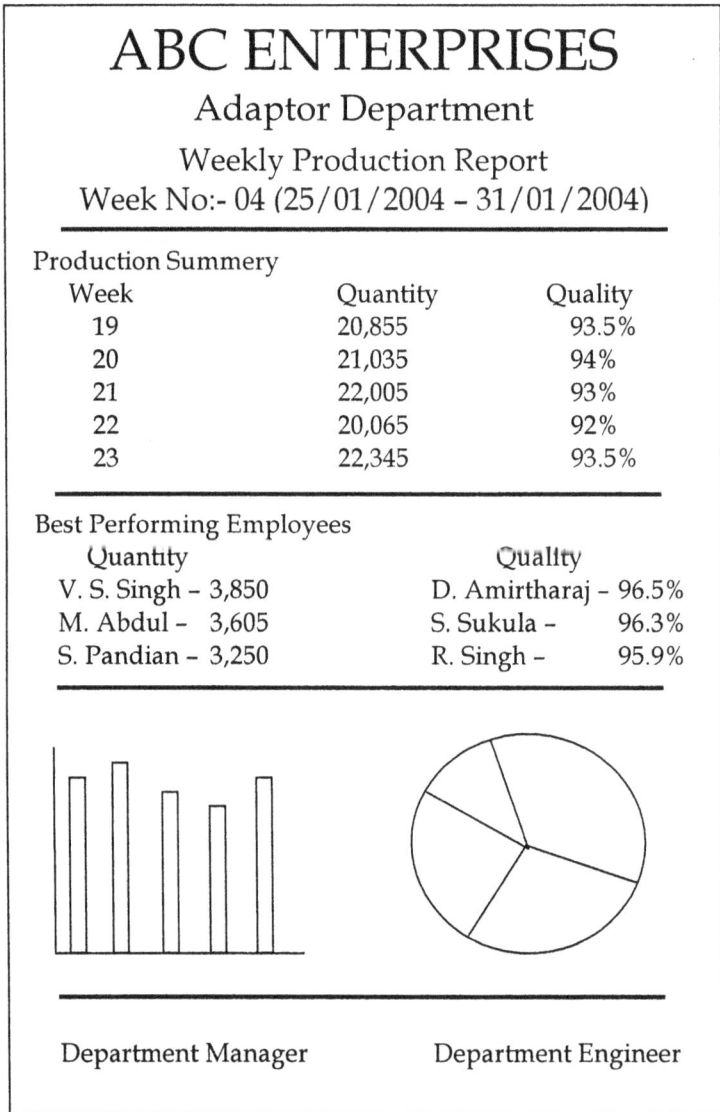

Fig 3.4   A Sample Report.

Chapter Four

COMPUTERIZATION

4.1 INTRODUCTION

Computerization studies how the usage of computers influences and changes individuals, groups, organizations, relationships between these social components and society as a whole. This field tries to examine and answer the following groups of questions:

1) What is the impact of computers on industrial production? Dose it improve productivity? Is it increasing the risk of unemployment? Do computers empower the workers especially women or does it actually weaken them against market forces?
2) How do computers help to improve service sectors like health care, educational services and government services?
3) How do electronic mail and internet influence individuals, social groups and human relations? Does it help to form new communities or does it undermine intimate interactions and lead to social isolation of individuals?
4) How do computers bring about changes in morals and social values? Do computers reduce privacy and personal freedom?
5) How can computers help us to improve the information management system and bring about a new culture in management practice?

Though the first four sets of questions discuss important information about computerization the fifth question how a new culture of management can be expected by computers is more important for this discussion.

4.2 ANALOGY FOR COMPUTERIZED IMS

The usual way to explain the influence of computers on the society is to compare it with what automobiles did for human civilization in the 1950s. Rob Kling in his articles explains how expectations about cars were changed over time. He says "When motor cars first became popular in the early twentieth century, they were viewed as a clean technology. Larger cities had annoying pollution problems from another primary transportation technology, horses. On rainy days, large pools of horse manure would form on busy street corners and walking was somewhat hazardous for pedestrians. By 1960s we began to view cars as a major pollution technology....." Car road analogy may be a better way to explain the expected changes by computers and the internet, but when discussing expected changes brought about by computerized information management systems, it may be easier to understand the expected changes through a comparison with money and the banking system. Enough evidence can be found that various forms of money and information collection systems have existed from very early days of human civilization. But until the 17th century, rulers of European civilizations were able to maintain their control over the society with law and religion as their main tools. Though various forms of money, banks and information collection systems existed at that time, they did not play any significant role in social relations or social control. But during colonization, when markets started to expand all aver the world, the need for a better social control was created. In 1602 the formation of Dutch East Indian Company signaled the beginning of the great expansion of market and Holland

and its capital Amsterdam became the centre of international trade. As a need in 1609 the Wissel Bank was founded to accommodate the needs of merchants by maintaining a true stranded of values in commercial transactions. But it did not give us a straight forward development of the international banking systems of today. During that time several banks including Wissel bank formed and dissolved with their contribution for both good and bad, to the credit mechanism of today.

Money and banking systems provide the best social tool for comparison and calculation. They have helped human civilization to climb several steps towards its success. However, the system has its own weaknesses as well. In addition to the risk of losing its value during financial mismanagement or mass production failures, we know that prices of products may not have a direct relationship to its quality. High prices do not necessarily mean good products and low prices do not necessarily mean bad products. So what is the ultimate tool of social control and what is the best way to measure quality of products and services? Here is the information that comes as an answer. If we can identify measurable properties for goods and services, then this information becomes an ultimate way to measure quality and such information-based management system will become the ultimate form of social control. Collecting information about several products, services and social relations, storing it, utilizing such information to improve human relations and productivity is a complicated task which will cost large amounts of money, time and human resources. This is one of the important reasons for the hesitancy to implement information-based management systems. But today, computers, computerized information management systems and networking facilities of computers including internet, provide an answer to this problem. The revolution which has taken place in information management systems has made this task much easier, unbelievably quicker and much more accurate. But money and banking system have made several contributions to human civilization they also faced several challenges for their development. In the same way, today information management system is also making several contributions and facing several challenges in its development.

4.3 SPECTRUMS OF SOCIAL SYSTEM

In order to understand how society influences computerization and computerization influences society, we must understand how each social system such as legal systems, religious systems, market systems and information management systems get organized into different spectrums. All social systems can be divided into four distinguishable spectrums. The bottom spectrum of all social systems is the practical spectrum, on top of it, lies the technical spectrum, on top of the technical spectrum the professional spectrum, and on top of all these lies the philosophical spectrum.

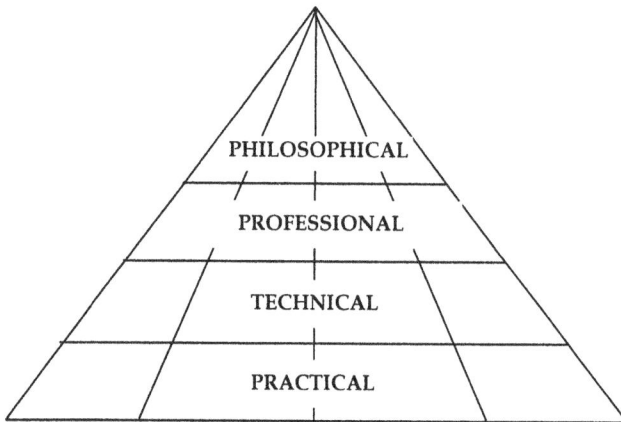

Fig: 1 Spectrums of Social System

Let's try to understand each spectrum in detail. In each social system the spectrum which is obvious and accessible for each and everyone in the society is the practical spectrum. Before the development of money and banking systems, important people in the society who provided services and influenced people's day to day life were governors as representatives of kings and priests as representatives of religions. They developed and performed several practices to maintain their legal and religious authority over people. Swords and religious books were carried by people to maintain their status and identity. Though money and information existed at that time, they did not play any key role in social relations. When money became the important form of social relations, every thing started to change. Banks and several other forms of market organizations became the important terminals of service providing. As money started to influence social relations, law and religion lost their significance. People started to carry a wallet or purse as their daily carry on. With the introduction of electronic form of money, a 3.4 by 2.1 inch plastic card became an important part of everyone's life. Once again the Information revolution is changing everything. Information providing organizations became important parts of everyone's life. The Internet and computers are influencing everybody. When managers want to make decisions, they are more concerned about information than other factors. Today pagers, cell phones, palm tops and many more electronic devices which can carry information have become important parts of daily carryon.

The next important spectrum of every social system is the technical spectrum. Before money and market era, kings and religious institutions maintained several technical individuals and technical institutions to support their systems in the society. While governors maintained soldiers and other technicians to maintain law and order, religious institutions maintained several kinds of technicians to support their religious organizations and various welfare institutions. When money and the market system came into existence, a different set of technical personnel were trained. These technicians printed and distributed bank currency notes, maintained accounts at business institutions, got involved in marketing goods and services etc. An information revolution is once again training a new set of technical personnel. Computer technicians to install, maintain and repair computers, data entry operators and a wide variety of computer technicians are being trained. This technical spectrum is important to maintain the functioning of the practical spectrum which lies below.

Professional spectrum is the next important spectrum of any social system. Important functions of professional spectrum are to create and maintain the institutional backbone and train personnel for each system. During the reign of kings and religious eras, we had ministers and their ministries to create and maintain law. Various types of educational institutions were maintained to train the required soldiers and rulers. Religious institutions also maintained several supportive structures to develop and maintain religious infrastructure and train priests. When money came into existence, a new set of professional spectrum was created. With banks and necessary physical structures, business studies, accounting studies and several other educational courses were created. Computers and information management systems are once again creating a new professional spectrum around us. High speed, big bandwidth information superhighways, internet, information servers, several educational courses in computer science and related institutions, as such a complete new set of professional spectrum is being created. By creating the necessary physical infrastructure and training personnel, the professional spectrum creates and maintains a back bone for each system.

On top of all spectrums lies the philosophical spectrum. The function of this spectrum is to create a culture for each system which will be made up of morals, values, knowledge and practice. Kings had several advisors and teachers who created and helped the society to maintain several mythological values and related practices on the basis of ancestors and natural forces like the sun, fire etc. Religions through their holy books and religious faiths created and maintained theological values and practices. When money and market economy came to existence, several political philosophies were created. These philosophies helped to improve several theological values, also created several social values based on market principles. Today computers and computerized information management systems are opening doors for scientific understanding of all other values and practices. The availability of a huge collection of information helps to break several unanswered questions about human relations and allows us to scientifically analyze these values and create a broad base for a positive knowledge about human relations. So it is the philosophical spectrum which creates a culture and values for every system which will guide and guard their course.

The discussion above on different spectrums of social system would help us to understand the challenges on computerization and development of computerized information management systems. The important information we can gather from this discussion is the expected time duration for implementation of new systems. As explained earlier the spectrum which is obvious and accessible for each and everyone in the society is the practical spectrum. Today people have started to see the advantages of this spectrum of computers and computerized information management system. It may be as simple as assistance in typing a professional letter or as complicated as weather forecasts; we started to see the advantages of computers. As earlier societies dreamed and achieved everything in the name of the king, everything in the name of god, everything through market mechanism, today we have started to dream towards everything through computers and the internet. Though we are able to see several successes towards this direction, we are faced with several failures as well. How long is it going to take to see a fully computerized world? What are the reasons for the failure and delay in this direction? To answer these questions, we should understand the difficulties in establishing the three spectrums which lie on top of the practical spectrum. To establish a computerized world, one of the important techniques everyone has to learn is keyboarding. To install, maintain and repair computers we need to train technicians. To plan develop and maintain infrastructure for computers and computerized management systems we need to train professionals and develop a complete infrastructure. To guide and control the development of all other spectrums we need a philosophical spectrum, that is, scientifically selected values, law and culture. Today we are facing several challenges on the development of each of these spectrums.

4.4 CHALLENGES OF COMPUTERIZATION

The most important challenge is finding the necessary resources. Though prices of computers have decreased over the past ten years, still they cost lots of money. As most of the governments and other institutions are running on tight budgets, finding and allocating resources to implement computer systems is a great challenge. For example: whether all the schools in the world are capable of implementing computer labs for their students, so that keyboarding can be taught to the future generation. Another important challenge on the establishment of each system is corruptions and mismanagement. The formation of Bank of Amsterdam did not give us a straightforward development of today's banking system. For failure of this bank corruption was considered the main reason. When an investigation committee checked deposit of Bank of Amsterdam in 1760, they could find only 10,000,000 coins out of 30,000,000 supposed to be there; that is 2/3 of the deposit was stolen by Dutch politicians (city fathers). Unfortunately, it was not the first time nor the last time government stole bank reserves belonging to its citizens. John Low created the Royal Bank of France, which failed because of loss of confidence by its citizens on its performance. Today information management system is also facing similar challenges. Computerized information management system has made it possible to collect huge amounts of information, store it and analyze it with minimum expenditures. This helps the creation of several information management systems which contain valuable and personal information of people. Though such systems are being created with good intentions, to improve productivity and enhance humanity, misuse of these systems were not uncommon. Several governments and institutions are being blamed for misuse of information management systems to interfere with civil liberties of their citizens. Stealing information form websites or from communication done through the internet is also not uncommon. Today, we can see that financial management has created a complicated legal system. To protect its function, we need to create a new set of laws to protect information management system as well. Today, we need globally accepted laws to protect information management systems, websites, and information shared through the internet.

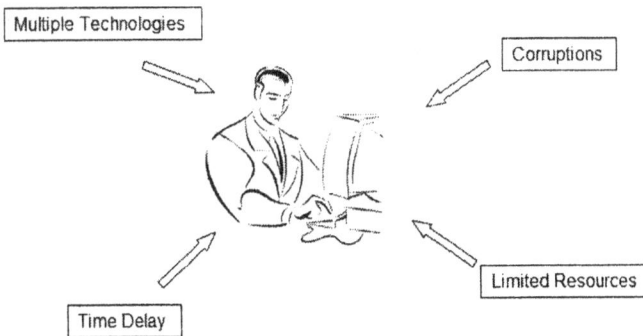

Fig 2: Challenges of Computerization

Another problem being faced is confusion over standards and multiple technologies. American banking system which was developed parallel to European banking system faced the problem of multiple currencies. Travelers across America not only faced problems on exchange of local currency but were also totally confused over the currency system of those days. In the 1850s there were 7000 different kinds of bank currency notes, in addition to these, notes also issued by schools, bridges and turnpike companies, railroads and other banking institutions. There were no standards; every bank found it necessary to use several bank note "reporters" and counterfeit detectors to determine the value of the notes offered at its windows. Several of these bank notes lead to failure. In the 1860s' several Acts in American congress brought an end to this confusion and brought standardization in American currency. Today we are facing the problem of establishing international standards for information technology as well. Though ISO and ANSI are trying to form a stranded frame, much more work needs to be done. The present way of achieving international standard through monopoly may not be the best solution. In addition to increase in price for the technology, it may prevent invention of better technology as well. Though creating an international standard for rapidly growing information technology will not be an easy target, development of an international standard platform will only help to achieve a stable growth for the whole system.

4.5   SOCIAL CHALLENGES OF COMPUTERIZATION

Another factor which was influenced by financial management system and going to be influenced by information management system is the basis and style of economic and social transactions in organizations and society. Before the influence of money was fully understood, the basis for transaction of goods and services in the society was done on the basis of kings and religions. Though various forms of money existed, they were used by kings and religious organizations to maintain authority, not as a property of public. When the money and banking system started to become public, the basis of social transaction was changed. Though legal and religion-based values existed, profit and financial advantages became the basis of social transactions. Profit and capital helped human civilization to create much complicated social organizations of old days. Though money has several advantages, it has its own disadvantage as well. It is not always possible to give a price for several goods and services according to their social importance or actual need for the products. Also as previously discussed, the price of products and services do not always relate to their quality. The information and information management system may lead us to an entirely new world of economic and social relations.

The new basis of transaction of goods and services is customer expectations not profit. Products and services are measured for quality according to their measurable properties. Quality management consultant Philip B. Crosby has an organized system to measure quality of products and services with comparable financial figures. The figures developed by him, Cost of Quality (COQ) and Price of Non-Conformance (PONC), give us a way to translate quality related information into money values. For example usually the loss due to poor quality of products is stated as 3-5% of production companies. It is just a direct financial figure obtained by multiplying poor quality products by their market value. But if we calculate PONC which includes all financial losses including customer dissatisfaction due to poor quality, the actual loss will go up to 25– 30%. In this way, the information management system is bringing a new way of understanding about economic and social transacting in the society.

Another expected change: increasing complexity of social organizations. As explained earlier, money and capital with their purchasing power enabled entrepreneurs to organize large factories. Entrepreneurs were able to build complex physical structures, buy machineries and large number of resources, hire people for money and organize the assembly line. Thus, money helped to organize complicated social organizations and helped to increase the productivity. The information and information management system is also helping us to build much more complicated factories and social institutions. Defined standards for resources of production, well developed procedure for production processes and quality stranded for outputs all these are enabling human civilization to form much more complicated organizations. This increases the productivity and the status of the human civilization. Expanding multinational companies nowadays may be a good example for this.

4.6   DISADVANTAGES

On the other side of the story, the unexpected and unwanted results of these social systems also need to be considered. When money and market systems were introduced around the 17th century in addition to the advantages, they brought several disadvantages as well. In 1888, for the first time the word "Unemployment" appeared in Webster's dictionary. Unemployment led to several other social problems like organized crime, prostitution etc. Today, we still fail to find definite ways to overcome these problems. What are the expected problems due to computerized information management systems? We have to accept there is always a risk of unemployment with computerization, in addition, increased sedentary life, prolonged use of the keyboard, looking into the computer screen may bring several health related problems. What is the answer to this problem? The obvious truth is as unemployment did not stop the industrial revolution or the money and market revolution, information revolution is not going to be halted by these problems. So we have to search for the solution within the industry.

Moreover, though money was created as a tool by humans for the benefit of the society, now it works as a social force which influences and interferes with everyone's personal life and decision making. Instead, human civilization uses this tool to achieve its objective; it influences human civilization towards a different set of objectives which may not be desirable ones. Likewise, information and information management systems also being created by humans for the improvement of the society; they may turn to become social forces which will influence human civilization. Another problem with each social system is over investment and subsequent shrinkage. During the peak of money and banking revolution, there were 30,812 banks in America, but after the economic crash in the early 1930s, this number dropped to 14,624. At the peak, there was one bank for every 4000 people, but this number dropped to one for every 8000. One of the important questions about the present economic recession is whether it is caused by over-investment in information industry. But if you closely watch the events you will notice the industry which is more challenged is travel and automobile industry not the information technology. In addition to direct challenges by the internet which tries to reduce the unnecessary travel, automobile industry is also challenged by the increasing price of petroleum products and increased safety concerns.

When talking about the delays and time frames, it is better to measure them by generations than years. When human civilization did not know anything other than kings and their rule, Abraham told us on the faith of the God that better civilizations can be formed. But it took more than 2000 years to form religions according to his expectations. When civilization organized itself on the faith of God, Adam Smith told us money and market can form better civilizations. Again it is taking more than 200 years to form an organized market system according to his expectations. How long is it going to take to form a civilization based on computers and computerized information management systems? Only future can give us the answer. With this understanding about information, information management systems, computers and computerization let look at what the available information of worksite is and what are the challenges in collecting and analyzing it.

Chapter Five

THE INFORMATION OF THE WORK SITE

5.1 INTRODUCTION

Information revolution is helping several different sectors of the society and lots of different functions of our daily life. With the increase of productivity in production sector, health, educational and government services also improve their services with the help of information management system. Computers are being used from running washing machines to weather forecasting. Though computers and computerized information management systems are helping us in numerous different ways, the scope of this study is to understand how worksites in production and service sector can be benefited from computerized information management system. As discussed before every worksite is made of much different kind of objects. Important among them are employees, resources of production, tools, furniture, procedure and products. In addition worksite itself can be considered an object which has important properties like humidity, temperature, etc., which may influence productivity.

Though all these objects have several properties, all of them may not be necessary for the management function. If you record all the properties of the objects and try to use such information on decision making, a lot of confusion may result. Identifying important properties of the objects which can influence productivity is a great challenge, which needs better education and experience about these objects. The greatest challenge will be encountered when you try to record information regarding employees' productivity. Each employee has several properties which are important to identify them. Some of these properties are important at one occasion while different sets of properties are important in different instances. For example heart rate and blood pressure may be so important for a doctor but his educational qualification and work experience are important for his worksite manger. Let us try to classify these properties according to their importance for management practice. Properties like name, facial appearance are important for identification purposes. Properties like address, telephone number and email address are important for contact purposes. Educational qualifications, previous work experiences are important for hiring purposes. Weekly work performance in production sector and monthly work performance in service sector may help you to evaluate an employee's productivity at worksites. While all these properties are important for different purposes, many other properties are not necessary, they may even be considered illegal to be recorded and used in management practice. For example an employee's personal interest or family details may not be necessary for management function. Recording their race or caste is even illegal for administrative purposes. So, whenever recording properties regarding employees, grater care should be taken to prevent collection of unnecessary or biased information.

5.2 OPINION VERSUS MEASUREMENT

One of the important challenges on collecting information regarding employees' performance is opinions about employees' performance and practical difficulty in giving measurement scale for these opinions. Let us explain this with an example. Nowadays many tasks on production and service sector are made up as a result of team work. To work in such team environment, employees should have very good interpersonal skills and be a good team player. In order to measure these properties you can give a simple measuring scale like (1) Unsatisfactory (2) Poor (3) Good (4) Very Good (5) Excellent and ask the team leader to record the performance of each employee. In such circumstance, you can see a measurement above 3 is always given for all employees. Rarely supervisors want to give a lower measurement value, in addition complaints may be received about biased grading given by supervisors. Though such measuring system may give you a general idea about employees' interpersonal skill, it may fail to give useful information which may help in decision making. If we want definite information which may help us to make a decision, then we should have a more detailed measuring scale. Table 5.1 may give you a useful idea regarding such measuring scale. Similarly any opinion on worksite should be given a measuring scale so that useful information can be obtained for management purposes. When establishing such measuring scales necessary professional bodies and university departments can be consulted for establishment of a measuring scale.

5.3   RECORDING INFORMATION

With regards to recording information at worksite instruments or tools called forms and check sheets are used for this purpose. These forms and check sheets can be created on computers with similar appearance and can be used to enter information directly into computerized information management systems. Forms are usually designed for the purpose of collecting personal and administrative information from individuals. These items of information are usually collected only once and do not change with time.

POINTS / PROPERTIES	5	10	15	20	RESULT
COMMUNICATION	Not a pleasant person. There are reports of poor communication by co-workers.	Not a pleasant person. Not tactful on communication. But there is no report of poor communication by coworkers	Not a pleasant person. But tactful on communication. Chooses appropriate word for a situation.	Pleasant person. Tactful on communication. Chooses appropriate word for a situation	
TEAM PLAYER	Reported conflict with other workers at work site.	Difficulty in get alone with others. But no reported conflict with other workers at work site.	Difficulty in get alone with others. But helps others to attain their goals.	Get along with others with very well. Helps others to attain their goals.	
COOPERATIVE	Reported conflict for changing environment. Complain on accepting assignment and instructions.	Difficulty in adapting to changing needs of the organization. Difficulty in accepting assignment and instructions.	Difficulty in adapting to changing needs of the organization. But accepts assignment and instructions willing fully.	Able to adapt changing needs of the organization. Accepts assignment and instructions willing fully.	
WILLING TO LEARN	Dislikes learning new things. Shows agitation on training in training programs.	Does not show interest in learning new things. Shows difficulty in training programs.	Does not show interest in learning new things. But learns new things easily.	Interested in learning new things. But learns new things easily.	
INNOVATION	Hides problems at work-site. Discourages people who try to help on identifying problems.	Does not identify problems at work site. Does not participate on solving identified problems.	Does not identify problems at work site. But works with management on solving identified problems.	Identify problems at work site. Works with management on solving identified problems.	
				TOTAL	

Table 5.1   Measurement Scale for Employee's Interpersonal Skill and Team Player

Fig 5.1 may give you idea of a form. On the other hand check sheets are used for the purpose of collecting information which can change with time.

ABC Enterprises

Employee's Leave form Work Request Form

(Need to be filled for absenteeism from work)

Employee's Name: _____

Employee's ID No: _____ .

Department: _____

Duration of Requested Absence:

From: _____   Till: _____

Reason: _____

(If for Medical Reasons Please Attach the Doctor's note)

Approval by Supervisor: _____

Approval by Department Manager: _____

Please hand over all leave requests to the department supervisor or manager. All request for leave should be approved by the manager. Non-emergency reasons leave request should be made two weeks in advance.

Fig 5.1   Form

These are mainly used for collecting information about the properties of objects which can influence the quality of the products. When measurement of these properties of objects are within the expected range they are called conformance and when they deviate from expected range they are called non-conformance. Check sheets can be designed to record both conformance and non-conformance. Check sheets used to record stock or the functions of a machine can be thought of as conformance check sheets. Check sheets recording non-conformance can be used for two purposes: one for recording non-conformance in a product and the second for recording non-conformance regarding a process or machine. A check sheet used to record the non-conformance of a product usually has four parts.

1. General information and information about the department
2. Information about the product and process
3. Records about non-conformance
4. List of non-conformance issues that need to be reported.

The first part, 'General information and information about the department' indicates the department using the check sheet and the quality checking section responsible for recording non-conformance as well as the name or ID of the quality checkers recording non-conformance.

The second section, 'Information about product and process' records product ID, processes that are being performed, personnel involved in the process, machine numbers used for the process and date and time of processes that are performed. This should make it clear that check sheets are not prepared at the quality checking point once the product has arrived but are produced when products are ready to travel through the assembly line. These check sheets should travel with the product and every operation performed with all the necessary details should be recorded on the production line.

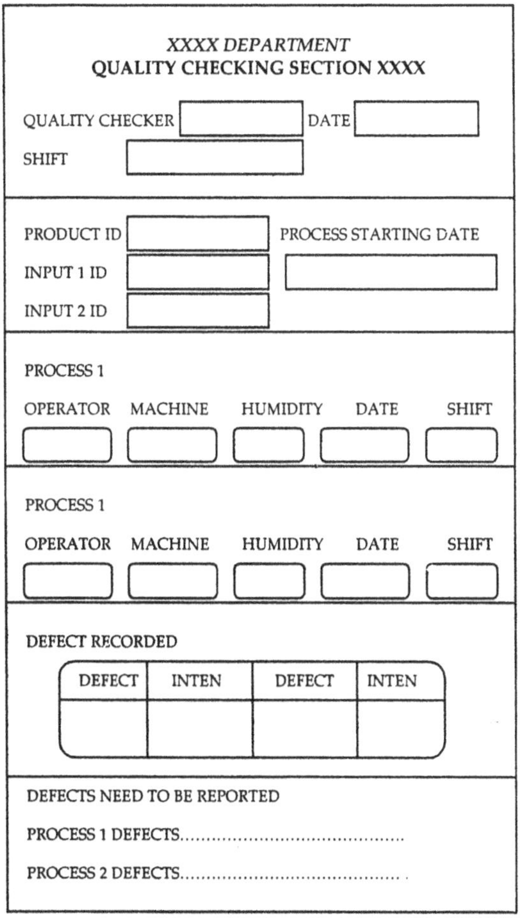

Fig. 5.2 Check Sheet for a Product

The third part 'Records about non-conformance' will be filled by the quality checkers. They will record non-conformance in the appropriate spaces. The fourth part will contain the list of non-conformance issues that need to be checked. Fig 5.2 gives a sample check sheet. When the products are small and a single person processes many products each day then check sheets can be prepared for a batch of products instead of single products.

Similar check sheets can be prepared to record the non-conformance of a machine or process. Here the structure will be modified according to convenience. A sample check sheet for a process is shown in Fig. 5.3 Check sheets should be designed by those who have a good understanding of the process.

XXXX DEPARTMENT QUALITY CHECKING SECTION XXXX								
QUALITY CHECKER [ ] DATE [ ]								
SHIFT [ ]								
PROCESS ID [ ]								

NON-CONFORMANCE NEED TO BE REPORTED	OCCURRENCE							
	DATE			DATE			DATE	
	SHIFT 1	SHIFT 2	SHIFT 3	SHIFT 1	SHIFT 2	SHIFT 3	SHIFT 1	SHIFT 2	SHIFT 3
NON-CONFORMANCE 1								
NON-CONFORMANCE 2								
NON-CONFORMANCE 3								
OTHER								

Fig. 5.3 Check Sheet for a Process or Machine.

A check sheet should record not only all non-conformance issues but also all other factors that can influence the quality of the product. For example, operator, machine, date and so on. Care must be taken to ensure that unnecessary information that does not influence quality is not recorded as this leads to time wastage at all levels and can lead to reduced compliance with data entry.

5.4 STORING INFORMATION

When the task of collecting information has been achieved the next important thing to be done is organization of information. Proper organization of information is one of the important requirements for easy retrieval of it in the future. In earlier days the task of organization data was done on paper based information management systems. Books named registers or records were kept in different organizations and departments for this purpose. Any attempt to retrieve information involves flipping page by page of these books. Nowadays computerized information management system, or more specifically Relational Data Base Management System (Eg: Oracle) are being used for this purposes.

As discussed previously in computerized data base management system information is stored in the structure called tables. One database can contain several tables which can be joined by primary and foreign keys. The following Database is a sample Database of a small department. Imagine a department, which takes two inputs, connector and terminal. They are being joined together by doing two different processes namely cleaning and welding and the output is called Adopter. In such department table named QUA_ADP is used to store information of the production process and important variables which can influence quality. Such table can be joined with another table QUA_CON which contains information about a connector, a starting product and another table named MACHINE which contains information about the machines which are being used in the process.

TABLE NAME QUA_ADP

FIELD NAME	DATA TYPE
PRODUCT_ID	NUMBER
CONNETOR_ID	NUMBER
TERMINAL_ID	NUMBER
CLE_OPERATOR	STRING
CLE_STATION	NUMBER
CLE_HUMIDITY	NUMBER
CLE_DATE	DATE
CLE_SHIFT	NUMBER
WEL_OPERATOR	STRING
MACHINE_ID	NUMBER
WEL_ROOM_TEM	NUMBER
WEL_DATE	DATE
WEL_SHIFT	NUMBER
QU_CHE_ID	STRING
CLE_DEFE_INTEN	NUMBER
WEL_DEFE_INTEN	NUMBER

TABLE NAME QUA_CON

FIELD NAME	DATA TYPE
CONNECTOR_ID	NUMBER
OPERATORI	STRING
OPERATORII	STRING
CON_HUMIDITY	NUMBER
MACHINE_ID	NUMBER
QUALTY_CHE_ID	STRING
DEFCT_ITEM	NUMBER

PRIMARY KEY

FOREIGN KEY

FOREIGN KEY

FOREIGN KEY

PRIMARY KEY

TABLE NAME MACHINE

FIELD NAME	DATA TYPE
MACHINE_ID	NUMBER
TYPE	STRING
MANUFACTURER	STRING
DATE_OF_PURCHASE	DATE

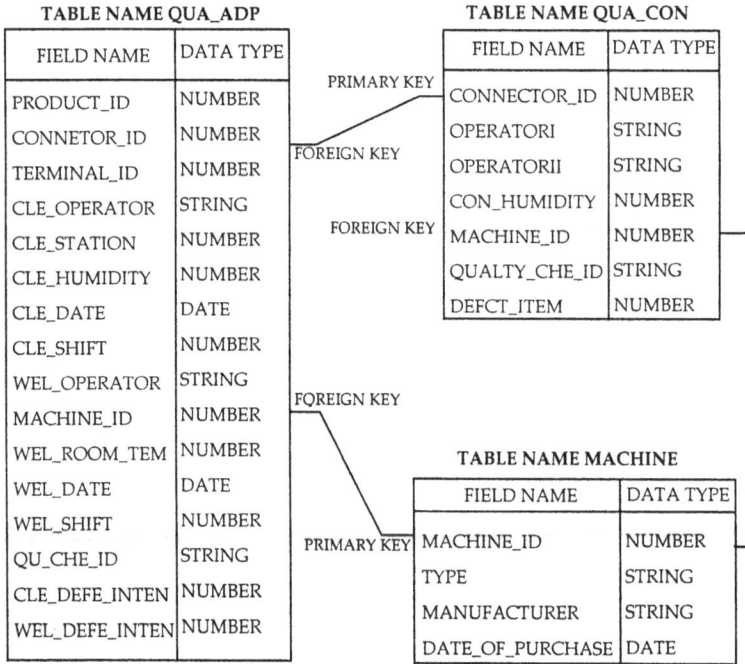

Fig 5.4 Sample Table Structure and Relations.

Figure of check sheet on 5.5 may be used to gather information for the above mentioned table of QUA_ADP.

5.5 RETRIEVAL AND PRESENTATION
OF INFORMATION

When the task of organization of data is achieved the next task is retrieval of information for the purpose of identifying causes of defect or other administrative purposes. Now let us see how to retrieve information from tables above to identify causes of problems.

```
┌─────────────────────────────────────────────────────┐
│                   XXXX COMPANY                        │
│                 ADOPTER DEPARTMENT                    │
│                 QUALITY CHECK SHEET                   │
│                                                       │
│   QUALITY CHECKING UNIT NO:-  07                      │
│  ─────────────────────────────────────────────       │
│   PRODUCT ID:- 9833431                                │
│                                                       │
│   CONNECTOR ID:- 9831031        TERMINAL  ID:- 9824321│
│                                                       │
│  ┌──────────────────────────────────────────────┐    │
│  │ CLEANING                                       │    │
│  │ OPERATOR ID  [        ]   STATION NO  [     ]  │    │
│  │                                                │    │
│  │ HUMIDITY [    ]  DATE [      ]  SHIFT  [    ]   │    │
│  │ ┌────────────────────────────────────────────┐│    │
│  │ │ WELDING                                     ││    │
│  │ │ OPERATOR ID  [        ]  MACHINE NO  [    ] ││    │
│  │ │                                            ││    │
│  │ │ ROOM TEM [    ]  DATE [     ]  SHIFT  [   ] ││    │
│  │ ├────────────────────────────────────────────┤│    │
│  │ │ QUALITY CHECKING                           ││    │
│  │ │                    ┌─────────┬──────────┐  ││    │
│  │ │ QUALITY            │ DEFECT  │ INTENSITY│  ││    │
│  │ │ CHECKER ID [    ]  ├─────────┼──────────┤  ││    │
│  │ │                    │CLEANING │          │  ││    │
│  │ │                    │DEFECT   │          │  ││    │
│  │ │                    ├─────────┼──────────┤  ││    │
│  │ │                    │WELDING  │          │  ││    │
│  │ │                    │DEFECT   │          │  ││    │
│  │ │                    └─────────┴──────────┘  ││    │
│  └──────────────────────────────────────────────┘    │
│   NON-CONFORMANCE NEED TO BE REPORTED                 │
│                                                       │
│         CLEANING                 WELDING              │
│       NO DEFECTS - 0           NO DEFECTS - 0         │
│    ACCEPTABLE DEFECTS - 1   ACCEPTABLE DEFECTS - 1    │
│    REJECTABLE DEFECTS - 2   REJECTABLE DEFECTS - 2    │
└─────────────────────────────────────────────────────┘
```

Fig 5.5 Check Sheet for Sample Data Base

When you want to retrieve information from a database, you have to give select query as follows:

Select {name of field you want to see} from {name of tables from where you want to select fields} where {conditions for records, which need to be selected}.

Here sometimes we don't need to use "where".

Let us see some examples of queries, which can select information from our sample database.

A] Let us begin with the simplest query- Retrieve all Fields from table Machine
Select *
from MACHINE;

Here"*" used to mention all fields and all SQL commands will end with ";".
Such query will give you the whole table of Machine
How to select whole the table QUA_CON?

B] How to select specific fields from a table with specific conditions for records need to be displayed.
Give Product ID and Name of cleaning operators for products having rejectable cleaning defects.
Select PRODUCT_ID, CLE_OPERATOR
form QUA_ADP
where CLE_DEFE_INTEN = 2;

Such query will give you product ID and name of the cleaning operator of products, which have rejectable defects. Such query may help you find whether the defects are associated with any specific person who may need further training. In such instances selecting all fields may be more valuable as it may give you any hidden cause of the problem.

C] How to select information about defects in product, which are produced, when humidity is above 60.0.
Select *
from QUA_ADP
where CLE_HUMIDITY > 60.0;
This query will give you all information about the products, which are produced when humidity is above 60%.

D] We want to see the following fields from two tables. From QUA_ADP table we want to see PRODUCT_ID, MACHINE_ID and WEL_DEFE_INTEN and from Machine table we want to see MACHINE_ID, TYPE, MANUFACTURER and DATA_OF_PURCHASE of machine used in production of each item. How to do this? Yes how to retrieve data from two different tables?

Select QUA_ADP.PRODUCT_ID,
QUA_ADP.MACHINE_ID, _
QUA_ADP.WEL_DEFE_INTEN, MACHINE.*
from QUA_ADP, MACHINE
where QUA_ADP.MACHINE_ID = MACHINE.
MACHINE_ID;

E] We have a suspicion that the defects in the welding area of the adaptor department may be due to some factors in the connector department. How to know whether there is any relation between welding defects and the connector department. We can select all the fields from tables QUA_ADP and QUA_CON with the following query.

'Select QUA_ADP.*, QUA_CON.*
from QUA_ADP, QUA_CON
where QUA_ADP.CONNECTOR_ID =
QUA_CON.CONNECTOR_ID, and
WEL_DEFE_INTEN = 2;

The 5 quarries discussed here will give you some understanding about query language. But query language is much more powerful than this. A good software programmer can give you much more complicated selection of data which may be useful in finding out the causes of defects. Any information retrieved from table with the help of query will be presented in structure called reports. Information presented on a report can be retrieved from different tables of a data base. It is also possible to include several graphs in the final reports. Fig 5.6 may give you a appearance of a report.

ABC ENTERPRISES
Adaptor Department

Weekly Production Report
Week No:- 4 (25/01/2004 – 31/01/2004)

Production Summery

Week	Quantity	Quality
19	20,855	93.5%
20	21,035	94%
21	22,005	93%
22	20,065	92%
23	22,345	93.5%

Best Performing Employees

Quantity	Quality
V. S. Singh – 3,850	D. Amirtharaj – 96.5%
M. Abdul – 3,605	S. Sukula – 96.3%
S. Pandian – 3,250	R. Singh – 95.9%

Quality Graphs

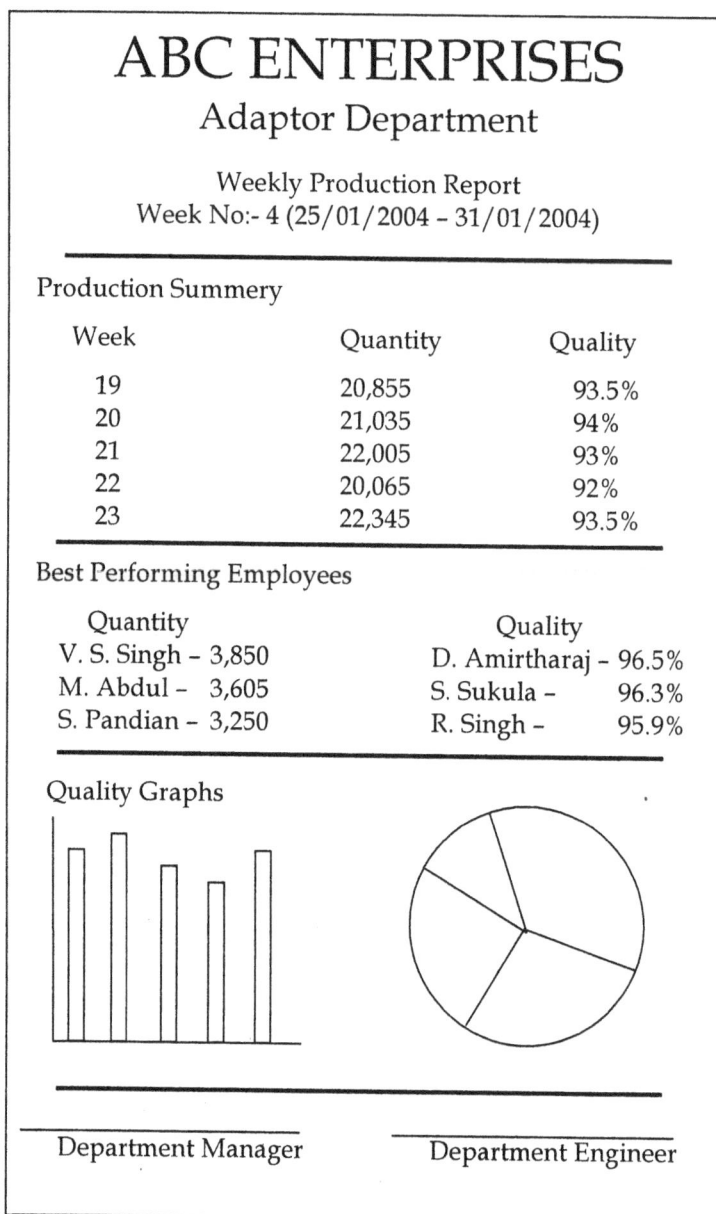

Department Manager   Department Engineer

Fig 5.6 Sample Weekly Report.

Chapter Six

MANAGING THE CHANGE AND THE FUTURE

Computers, internet, computerized information management system all are bringing about changes in several sectors of management function and human relations. These changes are bringing new transformation of worksites and production relations. A detailed understanding of these changes and better understanding of how to manage them are important for managers. Let try to list important changes occurring at worksites.

6.1 IMPORTANT CHANGES OF THE WORKSITE

1. **Increasing importance of information.**
    As explained above, computers and computerized information management system enabling us to collect much information regarding resources of production, products and services and utilize such information on increasing productivity. Though such changes are favorable for the productivity, people who are used to market and religion related values for the resources, especially for human resources may found it extremely difficult to accept any investigation and development of information-based management system.

2. **Increasing market competition.**
    Expansion of the market with the help of internet services, development in the third world countries and continuing liberalization of market relations around the world all are bringing increasing market competition for each and every product. This creates a greater pressure on industries to increase their quality and decrease the prices.

3. **Increasing price of raw materials.**
    Continuous increase of global population, development of the third world countries all these invariably lead to increase the price of row materials. This again increases the strain on industries to decrease their waste and improve productivity.

4. **Decentralized worksites.**
    Portable electronic devices, ability to share information through internet and increasing travel expenses all these make the old huge setup of offices or factories as unnecessary. As a remedy new smaller satellite offices or trend of working from home are increasing.

5. **Multicultural Worksites.**
    Another important change that is taking place arise out of multicultural worksites. Help of internet on human resource recruitment, decreasing barriers to travel and low cost of labor in third world countries all bringing this multicultural transformation of worksites. Though multiculturalism has several advantages it has its own weakness as well. Let's study this phenomenon in great detail.

6.2 MULTICULTURAL WORK SITES

As explained above one of the important realities of the world today is multicultural worksites and society. This multiculturalism has several advantages and disadvantages. Before going into a detailed discussion about these advantages and disadvantages let us first look at what we mean by the word culture and why there are cultural differences among societies.

6.2.1. Culture - Definition and Differences

The term culture may be defined as the "Sum of ideas, practices, and material objects that people create to deal with real life problems." Culture provides people with guidelines of behavior. When people interact according to these guidelines they form a society with a distinct culture. Within the word culture all the environment of the society can be included. All kinds of social tools like mechanical tools to buildings; norms values and ideas; social institutions like family to governments; even our dress all can be included in the word culture. Culture was created by earlier societies to protect it self from dangers and increase the comfort of living. Different societies in different parts of the world are faced with different challenges due to different climates, different modes of food collections, access to water and different challenges from animals. These differences lead to the origin of different cultures. When societies get better organized by kings and religions in addition to these differences several other differences also get rooted in the culture of each society. Today you can see major differences in culture is running through religion. The main reason for this, differences in religions originated in different geographical regions and religious books may be considered the first permanent record of cultural education of the society. These are the main causes of cultural differences of the society.

6.2.2. Advantages and Disadvantages of Multiculturalism

Multiculturalism has several advantages and disadvantages. The main advantages are people have opportunity to meet people with different cultural elements. This may help to form a better culture. A very good example may be numerical systems. Though many grate thinkers came from Greek and Roman civilizations their mathematical thinking was extremely limited because of the complexity of Roman numerical system. When they introduced Asian or Arabic numerical systems mathematical science took a leap on its advancement. Also though English is being considered an international language much of its vocabulary is coming from other languages. In addition to these there is evidence that, when properly managed, diverse groups and organizations enjoy advantages over those without a diverse membership.

While there are several advantages, multiculturalism also have its own disadvantages. The main concern is fundamentalism. Each culture has some cultural identity around which other cultural elements get distributed or explained. It can be religious or racial identity of each society. Whenever one culture tries to hold it vigorously and tries to impose it into other cultures then it becomes the cause of conflict between groups. Another problem of multicultural worksite is stereotyping. The term stereotype refers to a person's belief and expectations about an individual based on the individual group membership. One example may be blacks are slow and inefficient workers. Stereotyping leads to next problems of prejudice and discrimination. Prejudice is a negative attitude towards certain social groups. Discrimination is a negative action directed towards an individual based on his or her group membership. Stereotyping, prejudice and discrimination can lead to a vicious cycle. When management tries to discriminate an employee because he belongs to a certain group, an employee loses his confidence on management and gets de-motivated. As a result, an employee starts working slowly. His inefficiency gives the management the impression that just because he is from a certain social group he is an inefficient, slow worker. The management is prejudiced against him. It leads to loss of an employees' self-confidence and to a vicious cycle.

```
┌─────────────────┐              ┌──────────────────────┐
│  Discrimination │              │  Employee loses self-│
│       by        │  ──────────▶ │  confidence and get  │
│   Management    │              │    De-motivated      │
└─────────────────┘              └──────────────────────┘
         ▲                                   │
         │                                   │
         │                                   ▼
┌─────────────────┐              ┌──────────────────────┐
│ Management gets │              │  Employee stats to   │
│ more negative   │  ◀────────── │  work slowly and there│
│ opinion about   │              │  is loss of productivity│
│   the Group     │              │                      │
└─────────────────┘              └──────────────────────┘
```

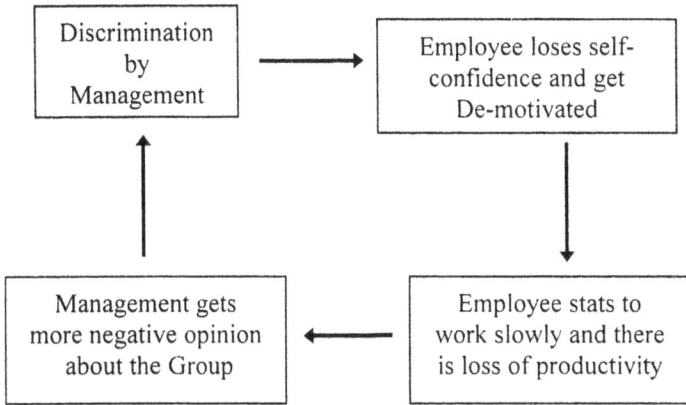

Fig: 6.1   Vicious Cycle of Discrimination

In a multicultural environment discrimination can cause grater damage to happiness and productivity.

6.3 MANAGING A CHANGE

Now let us see how we can manage the changes going around us so that best results can be obtained for individuals and society. An analysis of the problems towards change within a company will show that there are many points of resistance. There is resistance not only from management people but also from supervisors, the work force and even from unions. The reasons for such resistance are many and include social factors such as a tight system of beliefs, habits and traditional practices alongside personal factors such as rigid personality and the fear of being left out. To overcome such resistance, the following techniques will be useful.

• **Providing Participation**
All those who will be involved in the change, and all those who might be affected by the change should be allowed to participate in the planning and execution of change. In such a team every participant should be treated with dignity and

every opinion and complaint should be heard with a positive attitude. Working in this way will help to develop a favourable social climate for the changes that have to be made. Such teamwork not only prevents the feeling of being left out but also provides opportunities for the evaluation of the merits of the plan.

- **Giving Training**

It is better to train the existing workforce to implement a new technique rather than hiring or taking new people from outside the company. This not only prevents hassles inside the company but also prevents the loss of experienced and valuable workforce.

- **Education**

Education may be the most important tool in managing the problem of prejudice and discrimination. Prejudice like any other attitude is a learned behavior. So that education or better having a different educational system than we are having today will give a greater improvement on this problem. Basis for any such educational program should be as follows: Multicultural Society and Multicultural Worksites are unavoidable reality of the future. In such a situation prejudice or discrimination will only cause loss of productivity and loss of happiness. The only way to survive in the future is accepting this reality and learning to live in such multicultural society. It is worth to remembering some quotas from Charles Darwin. "It is not the strongest of the species that will survive, nor the most intelligent. It is the most adoptive to change". Any educational program planning for the alleviation of prejudice and discrimination should be instituted at multiple levels within the society.

- **Providing Adequate Time**

In all instances adequate time should be allowed for the acceptance of change. Indeed, it takes time to evaluate and accommodate the merits and demerits of change. Frustration and impatience at the delay in implementing change never helps; such attitudes may cause the resistance to become more acute.

- **Formation of Informal Groups**

In any cultural change, either inside a company or in society as a whole, informal groups can act to break down barriers and enlist the cooperation of all people. In quality management these groups are known as quality circles – but in society these groups can function under many different names. Informal groups work together on an equal basis to strengthen team sprit, help in the setting and attainment of reasonable targets, improve morale and communication, promote initiative and finally help to achieve the total cultural change that is being expected.

6.4 CONCLUSION

In conclusion we should accept information regarding psychology and sociology is not complete. Most of the knowledge we have can be taken as descriptive of the problem rather than analytic or explanatory of core factors governing human relations. At this point there is one important question. Whether using the incomplete knowledge of human psychology and sociology will improve productivity of worksites. It may be easy to answer the above question with an example from the medical field. Medical profession was aware about the disease tuberculosis for several hundred years. Until very recent time most of the knowledge we had about the disease were either some religious or philosophical explanation or descriptive information about the sign and symptom of the disease. The disease was well described; wasting, chronic cough, sputum, etc. Also we know about some factors which may be responsible for the disease. Poor nutrition, poor ventilation, overcrowding, poverty etc., are described as the causes of the disease. Based on this descriptive knowledge we were able to develop some treatment as well. Improving ventilation, improving nutrition also improving socio-economic situation condition, all these helped to manage the disease to a certain extent. But during recent time knowledge about microbiology greatly increased and eventually we found out the true course of the disease, that is *Mycobacterium tuberculosis*, a bacterium. Now the medical profession has a complete knowledge about the disease and also effective medication for the bacteria as well. Even now nobody considers that medication alone can cure the disease. Still the previous descriptive knowledge about the disease is true and important in managing the disease. Improving ventilation, improving nutrition, improving socioeconomic condition all are still considered important part of managing the disease.

The above example may explain how a partial knowledge can help us to improve the human living until a complete knowledge can be achieved. Though there is no complete knowledge in the fields of psychology and sociology, the available knowledge may help us to improve productivity and human relations. Even after core factors which govern human relation were identified, present knowledge may have importance on improving productivity and human relations.

REFERENCES

For a more detailed discussion refer to the following books and materials:

1. BLANK, LEONARD : "Changing Behavior in Individuals, Couples, and Groups" : Charles C Thomas Publishers LTD : USA : 1996.

2. BRYM, ROBERT J : "New Society : Sociology for the 21st century" : Third Edition : Harcourt Canada : Canada : 2001.

3. CROSBY, PHILIP B. : "Quality is Free : The Art of Making Quality is Certain" : McGraw-Hill Book Company : New York : Mentor Printing : January 1980.

4. CROSBY, PHILIP B. : "Quality without Tears : The Art of Hassle-Free Management" : McGraw-Hill Book Company : New York : Plume Printing : April 1985.

5. EGE, RAIMUND K. : "Object Oriented Programming with C++" : Second Edition : Academic Press Inc : USA : 1994.

6. KIRITHARAN, GANA : "Total Quality Management : A System to Implement" : First Edition : UBSPD : India : 2003.

7. KLING, ROB : "Computerization and Controversy : Value Conflicts and Social Choices" : Academic Press, Inc : California : USA : 1996.

8. MYERS, DAVID G : "Psychology" : Seventh Edition : Worth Publishers : USA : 2003.

9. SETA, CATHERINE E : "Effective Human Relations : A Guide to People at Work" : Fourth Edition : Allyn and Bacon : A Pearson Education Company : USA : 2000.

10. STUDY MATERIALS : "Advanced Certificate in PC Application" : National Institute of Information Technology [NIIT] : India : July 1997.

11. STUDY MATERIALS : "Oracle Hand Book" : Software Solution Integrated Limited [SSI] : Chennai : August 1998.

12. STUDY MATERIALS : "Computing Concepts for Business [CSI 1301]" : Ottawa University : Canada : Fall 1999.

COMMENTS

I want to hear from you!!

By sharing your opinion about this book, you will help me to improve my writing. After reading this book, please provide me with answers to the following 10 questions.

1. Your profession
   i)   Executive, Upper Management or Investor
   ii) Middle manager
   iii) Supervisor
   iv) Non-management Professionals
   v)   Student

2. How did you come to know about this book?
   i)   Advertisement
   ii) Training program
   iii) Friends
   iv) Display in book store

3. Your present country of residence
   _____.

4. Concepts explained in this book
   i)   Clearly explained
   ii) Need more explanation
   iii) Unclear

5. Illustrations and figures used in this book
    i)   Very Effective
    ii) Need more figures
    iii) Ineffective

6. Examples given in this book
    i)   Very useful
    ii) Need more explanation
    iii) Not useful

7. This book keeps your interest of reading
    i)   Kept the interest constantly.
    ii) Need improvement
    iii) Didn't keep me interested.

8. After reading this book, your knowledge
    i)   Improved well
    ii) Some improvement
    iii) No improvement.

9. After reading this book your opinion about profit and quality
    i)   Quality is of prime importance.
    ii) Both Quality and Profit are important.
    iii) Profit is the most important.

10. What do you like most about this book?
    or
    What don't you like about this book?

For contact information and info about other books written by Gana Kiritharan Please Visit:

www.gkiri.com

www.ingramcontent.com/pod-product-compliance
Lightning Source LLC
Chambersburg PA
CBHW032017190326
41520CB00007B/517